How Much Can a Bare Bear Bear?

What Are Homonyms and Homophones?

To my sister Mary,
who was merry on the day
she was to marry
　　　　　—B.P.C.

Homonyms:
Two or more words that
are pronounced the same
and spelled the same but
have different meanings

Homophones:
Two or more words that
are pronounced the same
but have different spellings
and different meanings

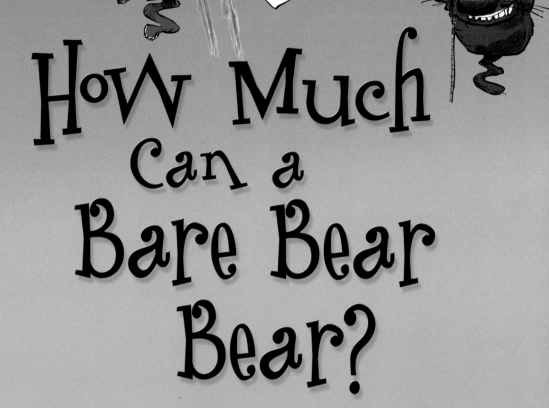

HOW Much
Can a
Bare Bear
Bear?

What Are Homonyms and Homophones?

by Brian P. Cleary

illustrated by Brian Gable

M̲ MILLBROOK PRESS / MINNEAPOLIS

Homonyms
are words that sound
and also look alike.

But they have different meanings, as in "Can you pass that can, Mike?"

Or "May I sail with you in May and coast all along the coast?"

These words are a blast
if you say them quite fast,

like

"Why don't we toast with some toast?"

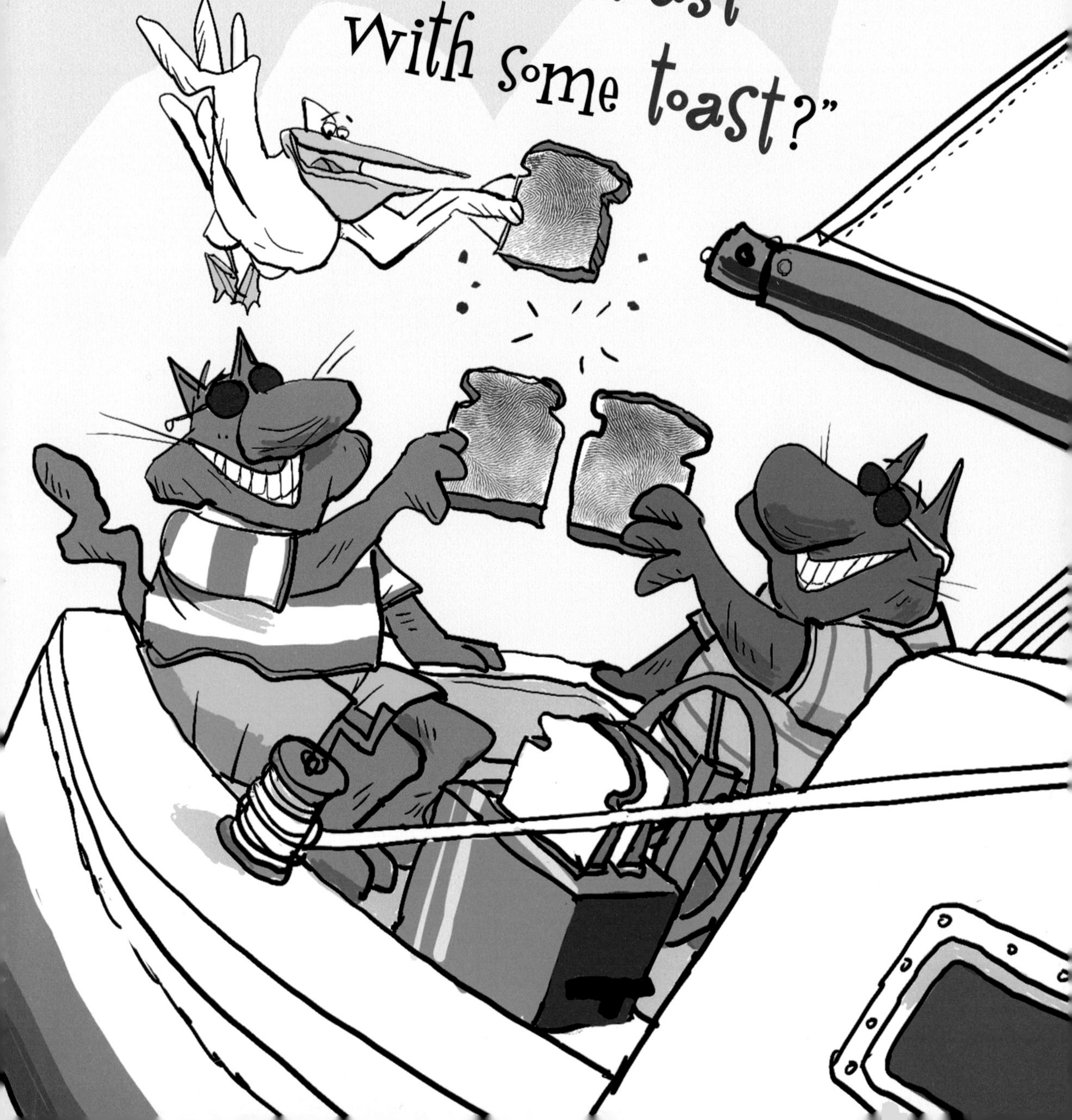

A light may be light, like a small paper kite.

A trunk can be found in a trunk.

An inchworm or snail could scale a scale.

A lean cat could lean on a skunk.

But punch cannot punch,
and at breakfast
or lunch,

your jam cannot jam on a trumpet.

Now, some words sound identical but are spelled in different ways. These words are known as **homophones,**

like
praise

and preys

and prays.

Though **homophones** have matching sounds, **their** meanings aren't the same.

And **there** isn't any question,
they're as fun as any game.

A horse can get hoarse
from talking, of course.

A ewe
could take you
on a stroll.

A fowl can be foul.

A toad can be towed.

An heir mustn't err in the air.

A Whale can Wail.

A male can mail.
A pair might just
pare a big pear.

A bust can be bused
by a driver you trust,

and Barry
can bury
a berry.

A band could be banned
if they get out of hand,

and **Mary** (who's **merry**)
can **marry**.

But the sea cannot see,
and it's clear as can be

that a ball will not bawl when it's rolled.

A moose has no use
for a bottle of mousse,

and a creek doesn't creak
when it's old.

But a **bear** should be **bare**,

and it wouldn't be rare if **Wood Would** be kept in a shed.

A Sioux
might not sue
if he knew
that the gnu that he bought
wasn't new like you said.

My niece could see Grease
both in Greece and in Nice.

A Czech could be
writing a
check.

A maid could be made
to be very afraid
when she heard
a big herd on the deck.

So, what are **homonyms** and **homophones?**

Do you know?

ABOUT THE AUTHOR & ILLUSTRATOR

BRIAN P. CLEARY is the author of the best-selling Words Are CATegorical® series and the Math Is CATegorical® series, as well as The Laugh Stand: Adventures in Humor, "Mrs. Riley Bought Five Itchy Aardvarks" and Other Painless Tricks for Memorizing Science Facts, Peanut Butter and Jellyfishes: A Very Silly Alphabet Book, Rainbow Soup: Adventures in Poetry and Rhyme & PUNishment: Adventures in Wordplay. Mr. Cleary lives in Cleveland, Ohio.

BRIAN GABLE is the illustrator of several Words Are CATegorical® books as well as the Math Is CATegorical® series. Mr. Gable also works as a political cartoonist for the Globe and Mail newspaper in Toronto, Canada, where he lives with his wife and children.

Text copyright © 2005 by Brian P. Cleary
Illustrations copyright © 2005 by Lerner Publishing Group, Inc.

Millbrook Press
A division of Lerner Publishing Group, Inc.
241 First Avenue North
Minneapolis, MN 55401 U.S.A.

Website address: www.lernerbooks.com

Library of Congress Cataloging-in-Publication Data

Cleary, Brian P., 1959—
    How much can a bare bear bear? : what are homonyms and homophones? /
  by Brian P. Cleary ; illustrated by Brian Gable.
      p.   cm. — (Words are categorical)
    ISBN—13: 978—1—57505—824—5 (lib. bdg. : alk. paper)
    ISBN—10: 1—57505—824—3 (lib. bdg. : alk. paper)
    1. English language—Homonyms—Juvenile literature. I. Gable, Brian, 1949—
  ill. II. Title.
  PE1595.C58 2005
  428.1—dc22   2004031106

Manufactured in the United States of America
6 7 8 9 10 11 — JR — 13 12 11 10 09 08